CHANGING THE ENDING:

BUILDING A LEGACY OF FAITH AS A GODLY FATHER

CHANGING THE ENDING:

BUILDING A LEGACY OF FAITH AS A GODLY FATHER

Lyndon Azcuna

Changing the Ending:

Building a Legacy of Faith as a Godly Father

Lyndon Azcuna

Awana Lifeline is a ministry of Awana.

© 2012 Awana Clubs International

1 East Bode Road, Streamwood, IL 60107-6658 U.S.A.

awanalifeline.org

awana.org

1 2 3 4 5 6 17 16 15 14 13 12

ISBN 978-1-105-71148-0

"*Changing the Ending* is not another program, strategy, or attempt at cultural reformation. It is a clarion call to men to embrace the scriptural blueprint laid out for fathers. A key component to avert God's judgment and ignite nationwide revival. This book is not for dads who merely want their children to survive the world in which they live but for dads who want their kids to change it! Reading this book will inspire you. To live it will inspire generations to come."

Byron Paulus, President
Life Action Ministries

"Every child deserves for his father to read this book. It simply tells it like it is. This is what God expects fathers to do. My compliments to Lyndon Azcuna and to Awana for making it possible."

Burl Cain
Warden, Louisiana State Penitentiary at Angola

"I have had the pleasure of not only working on the development of this book, but seeing the heartbeat lived out in my colleague and friend. This isn't just some thought-up, invented material on fathering; it is lived out each and every day and is an overflow of the passion Lyndon Azcuna has deep within him. As a father of young kids, I am doing all I can to build into my children and change the ending of my family's heritage. May you be encouraged and blessed by this material as much as I am."

Kevin White

Ministry Operations Manager, Awana Lifeline

"If you were to focus on one program and develop it in your church, your community or through a small group I would suggest beginning a group study using Malachi Dads. Focus on strengthening the hearts of children, enlist fathers to become the leaders in this process and you'll see generations transformed. I heartily recommend this resource, their small group process approach and the core of their message."

From the foreword by Ken Canfield, PhD

Founder, National Center for Fathering

Director, Urban Center for the Family at World Impact

This book is dedicated to my wife Julia,
who is my best friend, my soul mate, and the love of my life.
I couldn't be the man and father I am today without her.

Table of Contents

Foreword

"See, I will send you the prophet Elijah before that great and dreadful day of the Lord comes. He will turn the hearts of the fathers to their children, and the hearts of the children to their fathers; or else I will come and strike the land with a curse." (Malachi 4:5-6)

The closing verses in the book of Malachi are a rousing revelry to fathers of faith. The promise of a visitation by the prophet of Elijah was potent and prophetic, stirring the hearts of his listeners. But the most enduring exhortation in Malachi's message is linking two generations—the hearts of fathers and the hearts of their children. If this linkage is not successful, the land will be struck with a curse.

Today, both research and experience confirm that when fathers give heart-directed attention to their children, something intensely emotional and spiritual occurs. It's like a dad saying, "My calling is to make sure the hearts of my children are safe and secure." And when children experience this fatherly commitment, their hearts respond; they turn them to the hearts of their fathers.

Jesus modeled a fatherly connection to His band of brothers. In the gospel of John, He celebrates His relationship with His father using distinct phrases like, "My father and I are one...In my father's house are many dwelling places...I cannot do anything I have not seen my father doing…" Throughout the gospel He consistently references His closeness to His father and then makes this profound invitation to His followers at the resurrection site. Jesus speaks to Mary and tells her to, "Go tell my brothers that I am now returning to my father and their father to my God and their God." In essence, His relationship to His father was now accessible to His followers providing them with forgiveness, hope, and power.

In addition, Jesus modeled fatherly care through his ministry to children. He healed, fed, taught, and ministered to children everywhere. And he warned if any person leads one of his little children astray, they would experience His powerful wrath. His consistent investment in children sent a message to his disciples that children have inestimable worth and value. Moreover, children and childlike faith brought Him deep joy.

Welcome to the 21st Century. This will be remembered as a century where we will have to balance the deficits, become accountable, and face the scrutiny of God. We know in vivid detail what happens when fathers do not turn their hearts to their children. We know this is a curse, quoting Malachi, because a vulnerable child without a father is subject to a host of negative social consequences. We know that sons or daughters can become exasperated if their fathers abandon, ridicule, or abuse them. And we see the effects of maimed fathering in every community in America. It's not a welcoming sight.

Herein is where Lyndon Azcuna is called to action. His work in Awana Lifeline began in prisons, building a simple program which has been used to usher in "grace filled fathering." Their Malachi

Dads program that Lyndon spearheaded attacks the core of the curse with insights that will benefit fathers.

I have followed the work of Awana Lifeline and the pioneering work of Awana International for some time. Their vision and mission statement are compelling. Both Malachi Dads and Awana have the heart of Jesus in their ministry, and they know it will take a miracle to engage fathers with spiritual resources helping them create a Godly environment for their children to thrive. To that end they have given their lives to create a body of support that will aid all dads. I applaud their efforts and I am a big supporter of those efforts.

Here's the opportunity. We have little time before we suffer a total familial and social collapse. If you were to focus on one program and develop it in your church, your community, or through a small group, I would suggest beginning a group study using Malachi Dads. Focus on strengthening the hearts of children. Enlist fathers to become the leaders in this process, and you'll see generations transformed. I heartily recommend this resource, their small group process approach, and the core of their message.

Ken R. Canfield, PhD.

Founder, National Center for Fathering
Director, Urban Center for the Family
World Impact, Los Angeles

INTRODUCTION
Weaving of a Tapestry

Everybody has a story. Within our stories are ups and downs, twists and turns. All of what happens in our lives makes us who we are and shapes our being. As followers of Christ, we can look back and see how the elements of our life stories create a tapestry that Jesus has woven with our circumstances, choices, and passions. Our story does not end, and the tapestry is not a completed masterpiece until the day we leave this earth. When that day comes, it only ends our earthly story.

The most significant direction of my earthly story began when I was just five years old. My father died in a sudden accident, leaving me fatherless at a young age. When I was fifteen, my mother died, leaving a distinct imprint on the fabric of the man I would become. I had older siblings who cared for me, but the emotions that gripped me and the void I experienced left a distinct brokenness within me. That brokenness led me to make decisions that would help shape me into the man I am today.

Although I wouldn't recognize my brokenness until I reached my mid-thirties, my first defining choice came when I was seventeen years old and fathered a child. Instead of taking responsibility for that child, I walked away. My tapestry was being woven in dark colors until the Lord Jesus began weaving brighter colors into my life that not only made the present look better, but would also make a distinct and positive impact in the future.

It was in my thirties that I briefly walked away from my marriage and two young children. I was ready to, once again, make what I call a generational decision—something with impact not just on the immediate family, but for generations to follow. But just as I was at the brink of leaving my marriage altogether, God grabbed my wayward heart.

One evening while visiting the house that I had left, I looked in on my two precious daughters asleep in their beds. What the Lord said to me was, "You do not want to cause these girls to feel the same pain you felt as a fatherless child." My heart was broken.

God took ugliness, pain, and darkness and replaced it with love and passion for my wife and children. And my life that seemed to be unraveling in so many ways was once again being woven together beautifully.

Over the next few years, God began to change my heart in many ways. I began to think about the impact of fathers in the home. I saw that dying to self and dying to the world was pivotal in my ability to serve my family. I became intentional in spiritual disciplines and focused on learning how to raise my children for the Lord. Since I had no example in my own life of a biblical father, I looked to the Lord and wise individuals to teach me,. I have made, and still make, mistakes in this endeavor, but it is my heart's cry and passion to be all that God intends me to be in this area.

Today, as I work with Awana Lifeline, God allows me to use my deep passion for fathering with a group of men and children who also have been broken. The children are broken because they are fatherless. For many, their fathers are in prison. The inmate fathers are broken because of their choices and life circumstances, but it's no coincidence that the great majority of them also had no father figures or very poor ones.

Many of the ills in our society directly or indirectly correlate to the fact that fathers are not in the home, and if they are, they fail to have a positive impact on their children. The statistics concerning fatherless children are devastating. Consider the following:

- Sixty-three percent of youth suicides are from fatherless homes. (Source: U.S. Department of Health and Human Services, Bureau of the Census)

- Ninety percent of all homeless and runaway children are from fatherless homes.

- Eighty-five percent of all children that exhibit behavioral disorders come from fatherless homes. (Source: Center for Disease Control)

- Eighty percent of rapists motivated with displaced anger come from fatherless homes. (Source: Criminal Justice & Behavior, Vol. 14, p. 403-26, 1978.)

- Seventy-one percent of all high school dropouts come from fatherless homes. (Source: National Principals Association Report on the State of High Schools)

- Seventy-five percent of all adolescent patients in chemical abuse centers come from fatherless homes. (Source: Rainbows for all God's Children)

- Seventy percent of juveniles in state-operated institutions come from fatherless homes. (Source: U.S. Dept. of Justice, Special Report, Sept 1988)

- Eighty-five percent of all youths sitting in prisons grew up in a fatherless home. (Source: Fulton Co. Georgia jail populations, Texas Dept. of Corrections, 1992)

Throughout its history, Awana Lifeline has worked within prisons to help men own their responsibilities as fathers. When I began to see the changes God created in families of inmates who began to take leadership of their homes, I was amazed. The work of Awana Lifeline began at the Louisiana State Penitentiary where the inmates, because of their crimes, likely will never again have a physical presence in their homes. Yet they were assuming their God-given roles to be spiritual leaders of their homes—from prison! These men were directing their focus and intent on their children, giving action to God's work as written in Malachi 4:6a, "And he will turn the hearts of fathers to their children and the hearts of children to their fathers."

It was exciting to witness. The more I witnessed what was happening with inmates, the more I saw a disparity between them and free men filling the pews of so many churches. I began to ask the question, "Are the Christian men in our churches leading their homes?"

Today, Awana Lifeline is expanding to churches and communities to address this broad picture. What started in prisons is now impacting the world. It is my prayer that this book will give you a vision for your family, a passion to turn your heart to your children like never before, a renewed desire to follow God and His calling in your life, and a vision for being a Malachi Dad.

In this book are six principles to becoming a Malachi Dad, a spiritual leader of the home. Along the way lie the stories of many fathers with whom I have had the pleasure and blessing to work alongside. Those stories where last names are omitted are men who are living in prison, most of whom will never get out, yet are still living their lives seeking after God and striving to make a positive generational impact in their families. May these stories encourage you, and may God bless you as you begin your journey.

Lyndon Azcuna

Chicago, Illinois

Summer, 2011

Admittedly, the research on the impact of fatherlessness is a growing body of knowledge, with data that is still oftentimes out-of-date. Numerous academic, governmental, and non-profit research functions are continuing to address these staggering trends which will only provide us with better more up-to-date data which helps us understand the growing effects of fatherlessness. Regardless of the statistical notations, the Biblical call to godly fatherhood is a clear one – and the greatest hope for future generations is not found in the programs designed to address statistical measures, but in all men and women living their lives seeking to honor the Lord and follow His clear model for life.

Randy, *Malachi Dad*

As a Malachi Dad I made a pledge to glorify God and build His Kingdom by prioritizing the raising of godly children. A long time ago I realized that I had to own up to my responsibilities as a father.

My name is Randy. I have been a part of the Malachi Dads ministry since it began. Over the years I have experienced struggles as well as accomplishments. In the beginning of my journey, the struggles were many. Being a failure in my child's eyes was devastating. As the years progressed, I became better at fathering. I began to learn from my shortcomings and not dwell on them. I began to celebrate my good days with my son, and I noticed that he began to smile when he realized the person I had become. He did not realize that I had been working on myself for him.

When I look at him, I see all that God has entrusted to me. Every time I see him, I am overwhelmed with emotion because I realize there is no way that I can do this alone, no way without God. My son needs me more than ever, at thirteen years of age in these tumultuous times. I see a strong teenage boy with a beautiful spirit and a zest for life. He has a heart of gold and a compassion for people that fills me with admiration. He is meek with a quiet, reserved demeanor and a well-hidden sense of humor.

I love him, so it really breaks my heart to see him have to face the world alone. These facts compel me to pray for my son diligently. I cry out to God daily to confess my brokenness and inability to rear my son. Countless times I have begged God to keep him safe and away from harm.

I have prayed for his children that do not yet exist, that they be receptive to his leadership as a godly father in submission to the Lord. I have prayed for a beautiful, God-fearing wife for him. I pray that she finds the true love that only God can offer and that she is strengthened in His Word.

I pray that God simply keeps my son for His purpose. I pray from my heart that God uses me and my son as cornerstones to build a legacy of faith.

CHAPTER 1

A Godly Legacy

"He established a testimony in Jacob and appointed a law in Israel, which he commanded our fathers to teach to their children, that the next generation might know them, the children yet unborn, and arise and tell them to their children." Psalm 78:5-6

A Malachi Dad is a man who loves God and glorifies Him by building a legacy of faith in Christ within his family first, then challenging other men to do the same in theirs.

We all have a heritage. A heritage is, simply put, what we inherit. When we talk about heritage, we might be referring to physical characteristics, wealth, cultural heritage, or position in society. Every person is born with a heritage created by generations past. Our ancestors' homelands, our parents' careers, and our families' socioeconomic status when we were born are all aspects of our heritage. There's nothing we can do to change our own heritage; it is what it is.

A word that captures our hearts today is "legacy." While the meaning is essentially the same as that of heritage, it has drastically different connotations. We have the sense that we are passive recipients of our heritage, for better or for worse, but we can be active creators of our legacy.

Remember this attribute of a Malachi Dad? A Malachi Dad is a man who loves God and glorifies Him by building a legacy of faith in Christ within his family. He realizes that the greatest legacy he can leave is to love his wife as Christ loved the church and to teach his children to love God with all their hearts, souls, and minds. This is what he lives for. This is his greatest legacy.

The irony of this is that most Malachi Dads have not received such legacies themselves. Working with inmates across the country, I have seen the impact of fatherlessness as a negative legacy common among many incarcerated men. When I visit different prisons, I often ask the men, "How many of you did not have a father living in the home while you were growing up?" In my informal survey of groups nationwide, I usually find at least 70 to 80 percent of men raise their hands! It is not a stretch to say that fatherlessness has helped to fill our prisons. Statistics regarding fatherlessness in the home are devastating in and out of the prisons. It is a problem that runs deep and wide.

According to a 2009 Pew Charitable Trust report, "there are now 2.7 million minor children (under age 18) with a parent behind bars. Put more starkly, 1 in every 28 children in the United States—more than 3.6 percent—now has a parent in jail or prison. Just 25 years ago, the figure was only 1 in 125." The average age of these children is only eight years old, and compared to their peers, children of inmates are much more likely to end up in prison. I have heard Warden Cain from Angola Prison speak on this subject and when discussing this staggering trend he states, "If we prevent a child from following a lifestyle of crime we prevent one or more people from being a victim of crime, as well as cost to the government."

I want to challenge every man with this question: **What greater legacy exists than to influence generations of men and women to follow God with all their hearts, souls, and minds?** Is there anything greater? A spiritual legacy will last for *eternity*, *everything* else will turn into dust.

God is a God of generations. Another reason for pursuing a spiritual legacy in our families is for His sake; generations matter to our God. Read this sampling of verses regarding the importance of generations.

- "Now this is the commandment—the statutes and the rules—that the Lord your God commanded me to teach you, that you may do them in the land to which you are going over, to possess it, that you may fear the Lord your God, you and your son and your son's son, by keeping all his statutes and his commandments, which I command you, all the days of your life, and that your days may be long." -Deuteronomy 6:1-2

- "He established a testimony in Jacob and appointed a law in Israel, which he commanded our fathers to teach to their children, that the next generation might know them, the children yet unborn, and arise and tell them to their children." -Psalm 78:5-6

- Posterity shall serve him; it shall be told of the Lord to the coming generation; they shall come and proclaim his

righteousness to a people yet unborn, that he has done it."
-Psalm 22:30-31

- "God also said to Moses, 'Say this to the people of Israel,
'The Lord, the God of your fathers, the God of Abraham,
the God of Isaac, and the God of Jacob, has sent me to
you.' This is my name forever, and thus I am to be
remembered throughout all generations.'" -Exodus 3:15

When I first began to read about generational faith in the
Scriptures, I was encouraged. It seemed my children would serve
and follow the same faithful, righteous, and loving God that I
follow! Isn't that wonderful? But I began to read and hear about
large numbers of Christian youth leaving the faith when they left
home. How could that be? What about generational faith? Is
raising children to follow God a flip of the coin? Why were we
"losing" our children?

It is not the flip of a coin! Our God does not set a hope in His
Word based on luck! The key is *me*. *I* am to influence my children's
hearts to follow the Lord.

Of course there is no formula, no set of steps to follow that will
ensure that your child will, with no questions, have a vibrant, saving
relationship with Jesus Christ. Our Father does not guarantee this.
Indeed, many of the children who are walking away from their faith
do have godly parents who are striving to live a life that honors the
Lord. There are numerous factors that can impact and influence this.

Yet of greater concern to me is the high number of parents who
are completely missing this opportunity, this requirement, this calling.

What I *am* saying is that the Bible gives us guidelines in all areas of life, and this area is no different. If we read and study God's precepts, He will guide us through life, and He has not been silent in the area of children and generational faith. It is exciting to see what He says and what guidelines He gives to fathers.

How do you want to be remembered? And how do you want your children to live after you are gone? Wouldn't it be great to know that 200 years from now your family is living for God, in part because of the decisions you made today? I pray that we would be the kinds of fathers that cause those closest to us to see a light so radiant for God and His glory that they can't help but desire the same for their lives.

The power of parental legacy became clear to me when I read this description from Richard Mather, a great Puritan Pastor in the 17th century. He imagined unconverted children on the Judgment Day addressing their parents for neglecting their responsibility.

> All this that we suffer here is through you. You should have taught us the things of God and did not. You should have restrained us from sin and corrected us, and you did not. You were the means of our original corruption and guiltiness, and yet you never showed us any competent care that we may be delivered from it. Woe unto us that we have such carnal and careless parents, and woe to you that you had no more compassion and pity to prevent the everlasting misery of your own children.

I pray that this would not happen to any of us. It is heartbreaking to think that by neglecting our children's spiritual heritage, they would not enter into God's eternal rest. Let us fight for our children! We live in a world that may chew them up and spit them out with no care for their souls. Men, let us answer the call to be men of focus and passion towards our families!

At the end of our lives, we will not regret missed opportunities at having one more car, winning one more game, closing one more deal, or making more money. We will regret time not spent with our wives, children, parents, and siblings. Let us be men of the Malachi Vision. Let us turn to God and trust Him to guide us as we incline our hearts towards our children so that our children's hearts will be drawn to us and our Lord. That is what God's Word says, and we can believe it.

Miguel, *Malachi Dad*

Before I joined Malachi Dads, I had a very different definition of what it meant to build and leave behind a legacy for the generations after my passing. Naturally, my selfish nature inclined me to believe that in loving my children and their seeds of future generations, I should leave my own set of values and monetary support as my future legacy. However, after being introduced to the Malachi Dads ministry, I realized that the legacy I wanted to leave was a product of my own glorification and not of God's. I realized that not only was it selfish but also self-destructive.

I now strive every day of my life to be a Malachi Dad, not only to be a better father but also to be a better man of God. My striving to be a Malachi Dad is a journey to keep myself in check and lead by example, enabling me to teach my children and their children the nature and character of God and permitting me to walk in truth and teach them how to live a purpose-driven life.

I feel so blessed to finally realize my purpose, and I am now driven by this purpose; it's a love and joy to teach my children and their children about God's nature and character. So many of our children do not have a God construct, or they do not fully understand that God's nature and character is our model and that to live in His truth is to live in His likeness.

To live and walk in God's truth is our purpose and is the legacy we, as fathers, are responsible to leave behind. Our Father desires us to be like Him, so why shouldn't we have that same desire for our children?

The legacy I leave with my children is a legacy of love and life. If we truly love our children, we will desire for them to know true love and through this love give them life. The legacy I leave behind will bless my children's lives tremendously, will glorify God, and Lord-willing, will lead to their saving knowledge of Him.

"I have no greater joy than to hear that my children are walking in the truth." -3 John 4

CHAPTER 2

Man's God-given Roles and Responsibilities

"Fathers, do not provoke your children to anger, but bring them up in the discipline and instruction of the Lord." –Ephesians 6:4

A Malachi Dad is a man who embraces his God-given roles and responsibilities as the spiritual leader of his family.

The Westminster Catechism does a tremendous job of clarifying the primary purpose in life of both men and women: "Man's chief and highest end is to glorify God and fully to enjoy Him forever."

One way of glorifying God is to live according to His Word by fulfilling the roles and responsibilities He has given us. Men must embrace their roles as fathers. Though God may have given you roles outside the family—perhaps you are an elder or a deacon in your church or have a position of responsibility in your community—the role of a Malachi Dad is concentrating completely on your role as a father, husband, and leader of your home.

Do you know your role according to God's Word? Do you know what it is that God expects from a man who has a wife and children?

Because we oftentimes don't specifically understand our role or the responsibilities therein, we tend to "wing it." Sometimes we do know, but we are afraid to even try to fulfill it. We may not completely know how, or maybe we lacked a good role model and don't know where to start, or perhaps we're just too tired to make it happen.

In the void of our knowledge, experience, and intentionality, our culture defines and shapes what we do as men and fathers. Sometimes we don't know the Word as well as we should and default to cultural norms. For example, consider how we view money. Providing for our families is part of our God-given role. Making a living is right and good. It is a familial need that must be met. But does this need for provision include going into debt so you can provide stylish clothes or lavish gifts? We see other families in which children have state-of-the-art phones and wives wear beautiful clothes and jewelry, and we start to think we should be providing those same things for our families. Our culture often takes good things, such as providing for our families, and twists them into things that are not good. There's nothing wrong with having nice things, as long as you are not compromising God's standards in order to have them. But it's easy to start following the cultural definitions of "good," "provide," and "father" unless we are intentional about following the precepts of God's Word.

Take some time to reflect on your fathering role. Are you following the world's standards or God's? Remember, we need to examine everything in light of Scripture. We need to reject the parts of our lives that do not meet the standard. What is it then that we're *supposed* to be doing?

One of our roles as fathers is to be the leader of the home. We are to take full responsibility for everything that happens in our homes. We are responsible for the spiritual growth of our wives and children. In the biblical structure of the family, men are the responsible party.

In everything God created, there is a structure of authority and responsibility. God ordained structure of authority as the framework of our existence. We can see this throughout His creation.

In 1 Corinthians 11:3 we read, "But I want you to understand that the head of every man is Christ, the head of a wife is her husband, and the head of Christ is God."

As Jesus submitted to His Father, so women are also called to submit to their husbands. Our culture has abused this term of "submit" as well, but a careful reading of Scripture shows that wives are *equal people*, but their roles are *different*. Adam was made first, which symbolized that man is the leader of the home. He was made responsible for Eve, his children, and generations to come. In the eyes of God, there is a structure of accountability. This is seen very clearly in Genesis 3:1-13:

Now the serpent was more crafty than any other beast of the field that the Lord God had made.

He said to the woman, "Did God actually say, 'You shall not eat of any tree in the garden'?" And the woman said to the serpent, "We may eat of the fruit of the trees in the garden, but God said, 'You shall not eat of the fruit of the tree that is in the midst of the garden, neither shall you touch it, lest you die.'" But the serpent said to the woman, "You will not surely die. For God knows that when you eat of it your eyes will be opened, and you will be like God, knowing good and evil." So when the woman saw that the tree was good for food, and that it was a delight to the eyes, and that the tree was to be desired to make one wise, she took of its fruit and ate, and she also gave some to her husband who was with her, and he ate. Then the eyes of both were opened, and they knew that they were naked. And they sewed fig leaves together and made themselves loincloths.

And they heard the sound of the Lord God walking in the garden in the cool of the day, and the man and his wife hid themselves from the presence of the Lord God among the trees of the garden. But the Lord God called to the man and said to him, "Where are you?" And he said, "I heard the sound of you in the garden, and I was afraid, because I was naked, and I hid myself." He said, "Who told you that you were naked? Have you eaten of the tree of which I commanded you not to eat?" The man said, "The woman whom you gave to be with me, she gave me fruit of the tree, and I ate." Then the Lord God said to the woman, "What is this that you have done?" The woman said, "The serpent deceived me, and I ate."

What is the summary? Eve fell for the lie, made herself judge, ate the fruit, gave it to her husband—who also ate it—and their sin drove them to hide from God. What happens next is the key concerning man's role.

In verse nine we read, "But the LORD God called to the man and said to him, 'Where are you?'"

Even though Eve sinned first, God comes to Adam and points a finger at *him*, demanding an accounting. *Adam* was held responsible. Because Adam was higher in the structure of authority, he was ultimately to blame. God gave Adam the commandments and God held him accountable.

What is our takeaway?

The head answers for all those under his authority.

Adam was not only representing himself; he was the head of the whole human race. God takes headship very seriously as we read in Romans 5:12: "Therefore, just as sin came into the world through one man, and death through sin, and so death spread to all men because all sinned."

We can see the established structure of authority and how God reinforced it in the Fall. Let's look at how Adam handled the responsibility that God gave him. Adam says, "The woman whom you gave to be with me, she gave me fruit of the tree, and I ate'" (Genesis 3:12).

Adam blamed the woman God had provided him as his wife and partner! And we so often do the same thing. We grumble that our wives aren't keeping an organized home. We say that our children are not obedient or not trying hard enough in school. We whine that there isn't enough time in the day to accomplish all that we wish we could. Do we ever just stop and simply admit that it is, in fact, *our* fault? Only after acknowledging responsibility, can you pursue change through God's grace.

Genesis 3:6 tells us, "So when the woman saw that the tree was good for food, and that it was a delight to the eyes, and that the tree was to be desired to make one wise, she took of its fruit and ate, and she also gave some to her husband who was with her, and he ate."

Where was Adam during Eve's sin? Right next to her! Adam chose not to protect his wife. Adam was present, but passive and ineffective. He failed to protect his wife, and it led to devastation that is still with us today. Look around at your country and culture. Our failure to assume the roles and responsibilities given by God has resulted in nations whose god is anything but the Lord.

The story of sin entering into the world is a sad series of failures by both man and woman to submit to God-given authority. We need to do better in God's perfect strength! Because God's strength is made perfect in our weakness, this is a wonderful area for us to admit our inadequacy and call upon God's faithfulness to help us become the men we were created to be!

We are speaking in terms of fathers, but you don't have to have your own children to embrace the principles of living as a Malachi Dad. Any man can apply the Malachi Dad vision to nieces, nephews, grandchildren, and even neighborhood children. Of course, no one can take the place of a parent, but children without effective parents can thrive under the attention of a caring, well-meaning adult.

In all of these words about leadership, we cannot lose sight of the fact that we are talking about families! Husbands, consider your wives. Ephesians 5:25 commands us to love our wives "as Christ loved the church." When you start being the spiritual leader of the home, your family will more fully appreciate you, and you will have a sense of fulfillment as you act on this God-given role.

The goal of all of this is to impact our families and children for Christ. There are many how-to books about raising children, and you can purchase or download any number of activity-based resources. But is that all God is calling us to do? On a very practical level, it is good to spend time with our children. We need to take the time to do things with them that they want to do. We need to talk with them and get to know them well. We need to love them unconditionally. All of these things are good, but what is *best?*

The best guidelines *always* come from Scripture. What does it tell us? When you read Deuteronomy 6 and Psalm 78, it is clear— *we* are to teach our children about Christ. We cannot count on someone else to reach out and teach our children! It is not the Sunday school teacher's job. It's not the youth group leader's job. These teachers are great helpers to you, but they do not replace you as the primary teacher of your children! Your wife is an equal partner with you on this, but as we discussed earlier, you are ultimately responsible. Get comfortable with being your child's primary spiritual mentor.

God's words to Adam and Eve are echoing to us out of the garden: *"Where are you?"*

Men, where are you? Where are the Christian men working on loving their wives more? Where are the men who are raising children to love God with all their hearts, souls, minds, and strength?

This is our calling and responsibility. Ownership of this responsibility is the key to becoming a Malachi Dad.

On a final note: some readers of this book do not have intact families. This is certainly a hard situation for you, and your children are at a disadvantage, but this doesn't mean you can't impact your children. The Malachi Dad's vision took root in a prison—with broken men from broken families—and in the ashes of my own broken heart. If your children are products of a broken family, God will show you how to redeem that brokenness for His glory. Both in creative ways in your own family, as well as how you could possibly impact others in equally challenging situations.

Mark, *Malachi Dad*

I have been incarcerated for six years. I found my salvation and the grace and mercy of my Lord and Savior Jesus Christ while in prison. My relationship with Jesus Christ has changed everything about the man that I was.

I left my wife and four children alone and abandoned when I was arrested. Through my selfishness and lack of understanding, I was blinded to how precious a gift my family was. I also failed to realize the magnitude of the pain and suffering my children would experience because of my absence.

Through Malachi Dads, much prayer, and the study of God's Word, I have come to realize the full responsibility God has placed in my hands. I have learned that although I am incarcerated and not able to be with my children on a daily basis, I am still obligated to be a father—the best father I can be.

I have had the opportunity to participate in three Returning Hearts Celebrations since I've been in this insitution. All three have been blessed opportunities for me to reach out to my children and show them the changes God has made in my life. I have been able to express to them how important they are to me and that although I can't be with them, I do love them more than anything in life.

Malachi Dads is teaching me how to sow the seeds of faith in Christ into their lives, even from so far away. I now fully realize my responsibility as a father—to make sure that my children are walking in the admonition of the Lord. I now fully understand that these prison walls and the many miles that separate me from my children do not excuse me from this obligation.

If I accomplish nothing in my life short of making sure that my children know that I love them and that their salvation is complete in Jesus Christ, I believe that I will have achieved the greatest accomplishment any man could hope for. This is why I strive to be a Malachi Dad.

Jack Crans, *Malachi Dad*

I want to take just a few minutes of your time to talk to you about my ongoing experience as a father. Most importantly, let me commence by thanking God for my precious wife Sue, whom I married on May 7th of 1971. She was nineteen, and I was twenty years old when we committed our lives together in marriage. Now at sixty, I am still marveling in the wisdom and plan of God who, at the beginning of time, placed Adam into the wonderful grace of a family.

God's gracious heart in creating our three sons—Jonathan David, Timothy Paul, and Joshua Daniel—continues to be our song of praise! So as a father concerning his sons, please know that I recognize and honor the constant walk of faith that I'm enjoying with their faithful and wonderful mother. As Jonathan reminded us in a Valentine's Day present long ago, "The best way to love your children is to love their mom."

My own father is a veteran of the Battle of the Bulge, and by age twelve he had already given his father up to God's loving hands. Dad's loving heart always manifested itself with words of praise, fatherly prayers, and outstanding love for my mother who died in 1967 after a battle with cancer. At age eighty-six, he's widowed twice and spends his days encouraging his children and speaking of God's love for us through Jesus Christ. I still wear Old Spice because its soft fragrance continues to remind me of the countless memories of my loving, godly father.

I was once asked what one thing I did as a father that had the most powerful impact on my sons. My answer was, and remains to be, that I prayed with them and over them every day of their lives. I am grateful this very hour that each of my sons can remember the tender moments when I would kneel at their bedsides and call upon God for the care and embrace of their tender lives. Those prayers continued into the evenings of adolescence and early adulthood. I refer to these moments of prayer as "staying close in the battle."

Two important requests seemed always in my prayers and upon my heart concerning our sons: that God would create in Jonathan, Timothy, and Joshua hearts that manifested the qualities of both thankfulness and tenderness and that thankfulness would prove to be their response to the mercy and grace of God, and tenderness the quality of their lives in response to others. I can testify to the grace of God in answering these prayers as today each of our sons has matured into loving husbands, fathers, and servants of their Savior, Jesus the Christ. Jonathan is laboring in evangelism amidst the skateboarding culture, Timothy is a loving pastor, and Joshua serves alongside me in ministry to broken families of prisoners.

Here are just a few of the important things that I recall from when I was a young father that I know made a difference in the lives of our sons:

- Praying grandparents (and great grandparents),

- Daily meals together as a family,

- Loving notes on their school lunch napkins from Dad,

- Family vacations,

- Early-morning fishing trips and regular walks in the beautiful woods in all seasons,

- A dad who tried his best to coach and a mom who cheered loudly,

- Including them in the life of our ministry,

- Opening our home to the broken lives of children, youth, and adults,

- Staying close in times of challenge, failure or disappointment,

- Trusting them,

- Embracing the Scriptures as God's Living Word,

- Surrounding our children with loving friends and faithful servants of God, and

- Realizing our own frailty as parents while still seeking His fullest presence in our lives.

The Blessing by Gary Smalley encapsulated so well what our family has come to experience as true. The greatest blessing is that which comes upon our lives from the Heavenly Father yet can be lived out in our own lives with children and spouses. Here are the five behaviors of being a blessing to our children and grandchildren:

1.   Spoken words,

2.   Meaningful touch,

3.   Calling out strengths we see in our children and spouse,

4.   Seeing and declaring a bright future for those we love, and

5.   Committing to each one of our loves for a lifetime.

The Scripture that most describes my prayer as a Malachi Dad comes from 1 Thessalonians 5:23-24, and it declares my fatherly desire for each of my sons, my nine grandchildren and my precious wife: "And the very God of peace sanctify you wholly; and I pray God your whole spirit and soul and body be preserved blameless unto the coming of our Lord Jesus Christ. Faithful is he that calleth you, who also will do it" (KJV).

I'm writing these brief thoughts in the first hours before dawn. This special time of early morning allows me to sit in the quiet of His Presence. To my left on a little fireplace mantle sits a photo of my precious wife and our three sons. I know that my Heavenly Father loves me as I muse upon the precious family He has entrusted to my care. My heart is thankful, and my heart is tender to His mercy and long-suffering kindness in my own experience as a father. I could tell of struggles that every man would understand and speak of failures and disappointments without end, but I can also say with fullest joy and thanksgiving that I'm learning to rest in His love for me. The greatest blessing we can afford our children is to fall deeply in love with Jesus Christ.

In recent years I've come to appreciate the importance of intimacy with Christ, and I have come to know that as I see my own life as a maturing bride of Christ, it more and more abounds with the grace needed to be a Malachi Dad.

I've served as a prison chaplain for more than forty years and can testify to the sorrow and deep poverty of spirit that exists within so many hearts of fathers and mothers in prison. Yet I can also declare that God is doing a mighty work in turning hearts of these fathers and mothers to their children. I've seen first-hand the work of God in the prison where I minister and have been witness to what He has done in Angola (Louisiana State Penitentiary) as well. The heart-cry of the prisoners has driven me to hunger more and more for the love that I need in Christ Jesus, and I'm living to see the father-heart of God in many who serve in leadership within law enforcement and criminal justice.

I cry out to God that He will turn the heart of fathers to their children! I pray that God will visit this nation in His merciful presence and revive His work through the grace of repentance and saving faith. My hope is that single dads and lonely moms will turn to the living God and ultimately to their children.

In the tough little city where I grew up stand two iron bridges, one on the east side and the other on the west side. Between the bridges are myriads of broken families, illegitimate children, and perishing parents. Oh, that God would be gracious in turning the heart of fathers! There is no other remedy for this hour than for God to revive us again. The urgency is in our homes, in our churches, and in our own hearts!

After working in prison all these years, I've never met a life who needed Jesus more than mine. I lay claim to David's confessions in

Psalm 39 wherein he cried, "O, LORD, show me how frail I am and the measure of my days" (KJV). I embrace the words of Isaiah 66:2 that encourage me to know that God looks to the man who is desperate, broken, and who trembles at His Word. I run to Habakkuk 2:1 which so clearly reveals a man on the wall of watchfulness who patiently waits and looks to God for counsel and directing of His life.

On Father's Day many years ago, I took my sons away for an entire morning wherein I shared my father-heart with each of them. I shared my soul with them, admitted frailty, and also shared the important thoughts of my life. When finished, I gathered them all in my arms and prayed for them. While praying, I heard the crying of my youngest son Joshua Daniel. His tears were audible and almost overwhelming. At the close of the prayer, we all looked to him as though to comfort his sorrow, and he said, "Dad, this has been the best time in my life, and I'm only expressing tears because the morning together has ended!"

Oh, Malachi Dad, pray with your little ones! Embrace them, speak well to them, and by God's grace and mercy, may we all finish well, to the glory and praise of Him who so loved us!

CHAPTER 3

The Power of a Life Focused on God

"The righteous who walks in his integrity—blessed are his children after Him!" -Proverbs 20:7

A Malachi Dad is a man who embraces the power of a transformed life in Christ for his family to see and emulate.

Before we can be effective leaders of the home, we need to be right with God. We have looked at our major roles in the home and what God expects of us in these roles, but before we begin to lead our wives and children, we must be able to lead ourselves. We must first be dedicated followers of Christ Jesus—growing daily in His love, practicing spiritual disciplines, reading, studying, and meditating on His word. We must not practice it as a ritual but because we recognize that our hearts cannot grow without Him and His Grace.

In America, studies are indicating that 60-90 percent of children currently involved in church are going to walk away from their faith after high school. What is the number one reason for the departure of our children from the faith, according to the surveys? Hypocrisy, both in the home and church. Parents are not living out their so-called faith in the home, and our children are witnesses.

We have all heard the phrase: "Do as I say, not as I do." Most of us chuckle when we say it because we use it in a kidding manner. We know it's not a correct method of instruction. But we have to ask ourselves: Is that the way we're living?

We cannot expect our families to grow in Christ if we are stagnant in our walk with God. We cannot expect our children to live for eternity when we direct a majority of our time and effort toward earthly things. We cannot expect our children to serve others when we serve only ourselves. We cannot expect our children to love missions if we don't pray for missionaries in our churches or homes. We cannot expect our children to be the salt and light of the world when we compromise in our workplaces. We must model what we want to see in our children.

Throughout the Bible, God shows us great men and women living out their faith, doing what He expects to be done. Abraham believed God enough to take Isaac up the mountain as a sacrifice. Moses stood up to Pharaoh. Joseph, though wronged at every turn, obeyed God and did not become bitter toward Him. Noah built an ark in spite of his neighbors' taunts. In the first chapter of James, we are admonished to be doers of the word, not just hearers.

Deuteronomy 6:1-2 is a mandate for fathers to model their faith:

"Now this is the commandment—the statutes and the rules—that the Lord your God commanded me to teach you, that you may do them in the land to which you are going over, to possess it, that you may fear the Lord your God, you and your son and your son's son, by keeping all his statutes and his commandments, which I command you, all the days of your life, and that your days may be long."

This passage translates across generations as well—from grandparents to grandchildren, both sons and daughters. Yet as fathers we need to take the lead to embrace this mandate. Fathers are to teach their children to fear the Lord. How is that teaching best done? By a lifestyle! The following verses found in Deuteronomy 6:4-9 give us instruction about how to teach our children,

"Hear, O Israel: The Lord our God, the Lord is one. You shall love the Lord your God with all your heart and with all your soul and with all your might. And these words that I command you today shall be on your heart. You shall teach them diligently to your children, and shall talk of them when you sit in your house, and when you walk by the way, and when you lie down, and when you rise. You shall bind them as a sign on your hand, and they shall be as frontlets between your eyes. You shall write them on the doorposts of your house and on your gates."

The most important aspect of these verses is not the specifics but rather the lifestyle that is expected. How can we expect our children to love God with all their heart, soul, and mind if *we* don't? How can we teach or talk or walk or bind or write if it's not in *our* own heart and life? How can we teach what *we* do not know? How can we lead if *we* don't know where we're going? How can we give what *we* do not have? And how can we be an instrument of restoration if *we* have not been restored to God first? We can't.

If we are not willing to live the life we are encouraging our children to live, we are hypocrites. But nothing speaks as powerfully to our family members as a life totally dedicated to God. Children can see right through us when we say one thing and do another. But a life dedicated to God will speak volumes. Our children will say, "I want what my father has."

We are in a position of tremendous influence. We ought to live like we believe that.

Hayward, *Malachi Dad*

I accepted the Lord in my life in June of 1997. My life was a wreck, and I realized that I needed a help greater than myself. I had grown up in a broken family and never had the security of a good, two-parent home. Since I lived with my mother and five other siblings, for whom my mother worked two jobs, I pretty much learned to live and take care of myself, and was forced to become a man on my own. Our household was abusive and difficult to deal with. I never knew what it was to be a responsible father because I didn't grow up with one in my life.

As I began my long journey to recovery, I thought about my son. I hadn't seen him in almost seven years. I truly wanted to be a part of his life but didn't know how to start the process, especially because I didn't even know where he was. But I began to cultivate my relationship with the Lord and trusted that He would bring my son and me back together. I longed for us to have a relationship.

Soon after beginning my journey, I was introduced to the Malachi Dads program. I became a graduate of the first class of Malachi Dads, and I have been a facilitator in the program ever since. I learned so many things about fathering from a biblical perspective and about how God intended families to function. I grew continuously and continue to grow even now.

Not long after finishing the program, I was reunited with my son in a very powerful way. I can still remember the first time we met after so long just like it was yesterday. My heart was racing. I was nervous and didn't really know what I'd say to him, but when I saw my little boy, we ran to each other, and I just scooped him up in my arms and held him tight. We cried, and we laughed together. It was so natural for us to be together. It was easy, like we had never been apart.

Since that time, my son and I have bonded in a tremendous way. He knows the Lord and has been active in his church. I can't say that things have been perfect for us; we go through the same struggles as other families, but we have learned to trust in God and lean on each other in our weaknesses.

Being a Malachi Dad is a life-long endeavor of learning, experiencing and sharing the heart of God to your children. I am glad that I have become a Malachi Dad, and I'll be one until the Lord calls me home.

Preston, *Malachi Dad*

First and foremost, I have dedicated my life and time to become a Malachi Dad because it was time for me to not only become a better father but to become a better and more spiritual man as well. Since becoming a Malachi Dad, my eyes and heart have truly been awakened to the sinful nature that is inside of me. I am learning that my pride has hindered the healing process within me by hindering my repenting to God. God is so patient in me coming clean and owning up to the heap of sin I find in myself.

My intention and prayer is that I can take what I am learning and impart it into the lives of my now-grown children. I believe if they can see the change within me, they will accept what I am trying to teach them.

When I was free, my children were young, and my life didn't really have guidance. I failed to take the responsibility of being a father seriously. I did the basic things fathers do, but one thing I had never seen to do was teach my kids to be God-fearing people. I now know that studying and following the Word of God is a road map to a purpose-driven life.

I had to *surrender fully* to Christ and die to self by ignoring the worldly things that were once important to me. My *pride*, *shame*, and *selfishness* had to take the back seat; then and only then were my eyes able to focus on God and the things he had for me.

That's when my integrity and character in the eyes of other people began to shape up. I started speaking blessings and encouraging my friends and family about the importance of living a godly life.

Now I want my children and my grandson to be able to take what I am teaching them and pass it on to someone else. Now when I tell them God loves them and ask them how they know it, they will be able to speak from their heart that thus said the Lord.

CHAPTER 4

Our Poverty Before God

"For thus says the One who is high and lifted up, who inhabits eternity, whose name is Holy: 'I dwell in the high and holy place, and also with him who is of a contrite and lowly spirit, to revive the spirit of the lowly, and to revive the heart of the contrite.'" -Isaiah 57:15

A Malachi Dad is a man who knows how poor and dependent he is before God.

Look where God resides, according to Isaiah 57:15. He is in the high and holy place, and He is with the contrite and lowly. He dwells with us, and yet when Isaiah is in His direct presence in Isaiah 6, he is undone by God. It is in understanding how high and holy God is that we understand our own lowliness.

When men and women come to a correct view of the character of God, we see them become broken and contrite. It will be the same with us. There is no room for pride in a person who has a just view of the character of God. Look how these men of God responded after seeing God:

- Job, after hearing from the Creator, said, "I had heard of you by the hearing of the ear, but now my eye sees you;

therefore I despise myself, and repent in dust and ashes." - Job 42:5-6

- Isaiah, after seeing the Lord of hosts, said, "And I said, 'Woe is me! For I am lost; for I am a man of unclean lips, and I dwell in the midst of a people of unclean lips; for my eyes have seen the King, the LORD of hosts!'" -Isaiah 6:5

- Peter, after betraying Jesus three times, came face to face with Jesus' character and his own sin, and he broke down and wept bitterly. "And Peter remembered the saying of Jesus, 'Before the rooster crows, you will deny me three times.' And he went out and wept bitterly." – Matthew 26:75

There is no pride before the God of the universe. When we glimpse His glory and sacrifice, we see ourselves as completely broken and unworthy. David says this in Psalm 51:17, "The sacrifices of God are a broken spirit; a broken and contrite heart, O God, you will not despise." Proverbs 3:34 states, "Toward the scorners he is scornful, but to the humble he gives favor."

In another New Testament example, consider the Sermon on the Mount, recorded in the fifth chapter of Matthew. In this sermon, Jesus reveals what is expected of His followers in His Kingdom. Look at Jesus' words in the first beatitude, "Blessed are the poor in spirit, for theirs is the kingdom of heaven" (Matthew 5:3).

The one who will inherit the Kingdom of Heaven is the one who sees his spiritual poverty before God. We recognize that before God we have nothing, and that our righteousness is as filthy rags before the Eternal God. One must let go of himself to be able to be filled up with Christ.

A father who starts on the journey of building a legacy of faith in his family must understand that he is completely dependent on God in this endeavor. He must depend on Christ's crucifixion and resurrection power for the hope to live a godly life for his family. Only Christ can enable us and give us the strength and power to live this godly life.

Jesus continues His sermon by saying that the way into His Kingdom is through humility. Matthew 5:4 says, "Blessed are those who mourn, for they shall be comforted."

Who mourns? Those who have seen God and realize that He is truly high and exalted. When we look in the mirror and see ourselves, we mourn and weep. We realize our own sinfulness, and the sinfulness of the world around us. We mourn deeply when we realize how God intended this world to be and how far we are from God.

The next beatitude states, "Blessed are the meek, for they shall inherit the earth." -Matthew 5:5

What is meekness? Meekness is admitting to the world what you already admitted to God. You recognize that God is everything, and you say to yourself and to the world, "I am nothing." Meekness has nothing to do with weakness. It has everything to do with humility.

Jesus reinforces this teaching in the parable of the Pharisee and the Publican in Luke 18:9-17. Jesus states in verse 14, "For everyone who exalts himself will be humbled, but the one who humbles himself will be exalted."

This concept is also seen in James 4:6. "Therefore it says, 'God opposes the proud, but gives grace to the humble.'"

To be the godly fathers that God asks us to become, we must realize how poor we truly are. Alone and without His help, we cannot create spiritual growth in our lives or in the lives of the family members we are hoping to impact. It is all God's doing. We must begin with this posture before God.

Nothing brought this home to me more than seeing and hearing from a repentant inmate father who understood his sins as first and foremost an affront to God. He truly understands his brokenness before God. Because he is in prison, his surroundings will remind him of his sins every day for the rest of his life. But this same man also has come to understand his role as spiritual leader of his home. He is completely dependent on God to work in a home that he will never again inhabit. Although limited, this inmate is honoring the Lord by doing what he can to influence his family from behind bars. God works with the broken and contrite.

So, how about us? Most of us are in homes with our families every day, but are we broken enough to see our failings and to lean completely on God? Can we humble ourselves enough to let Him have all the glory and change our hearts and the hearts of those around us? I pray it is so.

Some fathers may not be in homes with their families because of marital problems. If you are like I was and not yet divorced, is there a way God can restore your home? Ask Him to help you to follow His heart and heal you and your family. If there is no way to live as one unit with your family, then rely on God's guidance for how to yet be the father He is asking you to be.

We need to see God for who He is—a holy and righteous God. As I said earlier, I walked away from my wife seven years into my marriage, leaving my two darling girls. But I saw how dark I was and how holy God is. Through God's grace working in my life, I repented and turned from my sin. And I was never the same again.

Jesse, *Malachi Dad*

First I give obedience to God who is worthy of all praise. I have only been participating in Malachi Dads for a few weeks, and already I wish for more involvement. Up to this point, I have learned that in seeking Him you must be truly dedicated. Malachi Dads has moved my soul in the direction of searching for Christ wholeheartedly. I truly want to walk for Christ and Christ alone. I have discovered, through the help of the Malachi Dads Program, many facets of my lifestyle that desperately need improvement. I do believe in Christ Jesus, and I do believe that He will continue to lead me along the way. I just ask God to give me the desire and power to continue seeking Him. I know that I need Him and will always need Him. My walk hasn't been easy at all, but all glory to God, I am still standing and will continue to stand for Christ.

Malachi Dads has taught me to be submissive and obedient to God. I must not continue living for self. The self must die to Christ so that I may live for Christ. I must let go of many things in my life in order to do this. I must break up the hard ground to allow God to work in my spiritual life. I am willing to allow God to break me and draw me closer to Him. I seek to bring forth good fruit in the lives of my family and my children as well as those who surround me. I ask that God make me a productive Christian doing His will. We must love and put God first and foremost in our lives and everything we do. We must be reminded to return to Christ, our first love. Not because we choose to or choose God, but because He first chose us. God is the truth, the light, and the love that we all need in our everyday lives.

We cannot walk around living a prideful life. Pride will keep us at a distance from God. We must put our pride aside and humble ourselves under God's grace and power. The world admires the self-confident, the ambitious, and even the proud. Therefore we must not exalt ourselves but instead allow the mighty power of God to work within us. As long as we continue to strive forward, God will continue to peel away the layers of pride and disobedience. Pride is evil, and anything that is evil is of the devil. We must confront our sins before God. We must ask for and receive His forgiveness.

As I continue to participate in this study, I hope to be brought closer to God. I hope to instill the real rest of God within my children so they may seek Him and to the rest of the generations so they may seek Him as well. I look for a better relationship with Christ, my children, and also my family. My name is Jesse, I'm twenty-five years old, and I will continue to seek God faithfully. I encourage others to participate in Malachi Dads and other godly worship. God is the beginning and will be the end.

Brandon, *Malachi Dad*

In building a legacy of faith, I pray daily that God will use me and give me the faith that I need to become a Malachi Dad. I have faith, and I'm working on building it further. Owning our responsibility as fathers is hard at times; I cannot control the things in my children's lives. But I seek to have a great influence over my children. I communicate with them through letters and during visits, but I only see my daughter. I have yet to see my son since 2008. Despite this setback, each and every time I see my daughter, we talk about things that are going on in her life.

I allow her to speak and to ask questions about the things that she wants to know. And even though I'm incarcerated, I try my best to provide for my children, even if it comes through someone else. I feel like it's my responsibility because I left them out there, and they did not ask to come into this world. I always try my best to give my children advice on how to succeed in the choices they make in life.

Understanding our poverty before God: this is an area that I understand, but am still growing. I work daily to further understand the power of the gospel. It gets rough at times due to the conditions we're living under. But I attempt to do what I know is both right and pleasing in God's eyes. I do my best to stay away from that which is not right.

Dying to self comes in to play here. Though I have certainly not finished my journey, I am closer to my goal as each day passes. This journey, this mission, becomes all the easier when lived in the light of the Lord. Though faced with great adversity in my surroundings, I must simply ask myself what God wishes for me to do, and I do everything for Him.

CHAPTER 5

The Power of the Gospel

"For I am not ashamed of the gospel, for it is the power of God for salvation to everyone who believes, to the Jew first and also to the Greek. For in it the righteousness of God is revealed from faith for faith, as it is written, 'The righteous shall live by faith.'" -Romans 1:16-17

A Malachi Dad is a man who lives by the Gospel, being aware daily of his need for salvation and sanctification.

A Malachi Dad does not drift lazily, hoping that God will use him from time to time. A Malachi Dad considers God's expectations for him as he tries to manifest God's example to his family. The Word of God raises the bar extremely high. Matthew 5:48 tells us, "You therefore must be perfect, as your heavenly Father is perfect." God expects us to be perfect? How on earth do we achieve this?

Therein lies the power of the Gospel! We obviously are not perfect in and of ourselves; it is only through Christ that we can be holy. Holy—set apart—as Paul expresses in 2 Timothy 2:21: "he will be a vessel for honorable use, set apart as holy, useful to the master of the house, ready for every good work." It is only through the

Gospel that we can be the men—the husbands and fathers—God wants us to be.

But what is the Gospel? The Gospel is more than a ticket to heaven, and the response to it is more than a prayer we and our kids recite when ready to accept Christ as Savior. It is more than that! It is life. It is the absolute solution for our brokenness. It is our need for God and our dependence on Him for all things.

This is why the Bible calls fathers to preach the Gospel to their children *every day*. Because it is their life! Every moment of every day is an opportunity to live the Gospel and pass it on to the next generation. The psalmist, in Psalm 78:5-7, explains that God *commands* fathers to teach His statutes and laws to the next generation so that they will put their trust in Him, not forget His deeds, and keep His commands. Ephesians 6:4 tells fathers to bring their children up in the training and instruction of the Lord. Being taught and trained consistently gives children a true understanding of the Gospel.

The Gospel shows who God is and what He's done for us. John, in John 1:14, touches on the enormity of the gospel: "And the Word became flesh and dwelt among us, and we have seen his glory, glory as of the only Son from the Father, full of grace and truth." God became flesh, became a man, and came to live among us. He descended from His throne and from greatness we cannot even imagine to live with us, to be one of us! Paul explains in Philippians 2:6-7 that Jesus completely let go of His right and even His nature by becoming one of us, and if that weren't enough, verse 8 goes on to say, "And being found in human form, he humbled himself by becoming obedient to the point of death, even death on a cross." *This* is what we need to explain as leaders of the home.

The resurrected Christ living in and through us allows us to become the godly men God has called us to be. The Gospel gives us the power to deny our earthly ambitions and accept our heavenly prizes, to deny vain praises of men and accept our fear of God, to deny the emptiness of this world and accept our fullness in the presence of God!

Christ is my sanctification. As stated in 1 Corinthians 1:30, "And because of him you are in Christ Jesus, who became to us wisdom from God, righteousness and sanctification and redemption." The apostle Paul said it well in Romans 7:24-25, after expressing his struggle in the Christian life, when he said, "Wretched man that I am! Who will deliver me from this body of death? Thanks be to God through Jesus Christ our Lord! So then, I myself serve the law of God with my mind, but with my flesh I serve the law of sin."

Paul is asking who will save him from his desperate situation. We have all felt a similar desperation, and it often embodies itself in our parenting. Like Paul, we need to look to Jesus for the answer to our desperation.

Jesus Christ is always the answer; the problem is not precisely what we do or don't do but rather what drives our choices—our sinful nature. You might say that the problem is not in the fruit (actions, attitudes) but in the root (sinful nature of man). The heart is the issue. Therefore, Christ is the only answer in helping men to be godly fathers. We must acquaint ourselves deeply with the Gospel, in knowledge and in life. This Gospel does not just save us from eternal death—it saves us from a meaningless life!

Larry, *Malachi Dad*

My name is Larry, and my involvement with Malachi Dads is very personal. First and foremost, I decided to become a Malachi Dad because I needed to know and understand the works of God. I also wanted to become a better person not only for myself but for my family and the people around me. My life hasn't been all that splendid and certainly not righteous. I never truly understood what God had planned for me or how to begin living a life of love. I always felt that I was meant to live just as I pleased and didn't know what it was to put my trust in God.

The people that I loved were taken away from me, and everything I did failed while all else was lost. I continued to live the ways of the world by lying, cheating, and hurting people that never did me any harm because I took no responsibility and refused to place myself at fault. Through all of my mess I produced two kids, and suddenly my life was more confused and troubled than ever; my selfish behavior became more rampant, and I didn't know if I could handle being responsible for somebody else's life.

I began to indulge myself still more into the world, and my life of selfish pleasure eventually landed me in jail. But I didn't stop there. I continued to do what I felt was right, but in the inside my heart was crying out for love. I was broken inside and didn't know where my life was heading. As time passed I became involved in a few Bible study courses, at which time God started to reveal His self to me through other people. I began to understand that God had a purpose for my life and despite it all He loved me still.

When I heard about the Malachi Dads and its purpose, I decided to attend the program. Since beginning the course, I've discovered what it means to be a Malachi Dad and what God has in store for me and for my life. So now I'm striving to become a more responsible person—not only for myself but also for my kids, my family, and generation to come. In the end, I wish only to become more intimate with God and do His will.

Jeremy, *Malachi Dad*

My name is Jeremy, and I am a Malachi Dad. I am one of many fathers building a legacy of faith from inside prison.

As a Malachi Dad, I strive day after day to become closer to God. I want not only my walk to be accounted for, but my children's walks also.

In building and maintaining relationship, you only receive that which you give. I grew up not knowing my father. Life was very hard for me without a positive role model. For this reason, I embrace the lifestyle of a Malachi Dad and own up to my responsibility as a father.

I teach my children about our Lord and Savior and the love He has for us as children. I encourage them to love their neighbors as themselves. They have also learned the impossibility of perfection and the inevitability of sin, but I have also taught them to repent for their sins and receive God's forgiveness.

Being a Malachi Dad has really opened my eyes to the power of the Gospel and has opened my heart to my children in ways I wish my father could have done for me.

CHAPTER 6

Dying Daily to Self

"And He said to all, 'If anyone would come after me, let him deny himself and take up his cross daily and follow me.'" -Luke 9:23

A Malachi Dad is a man who dies to self, daily.

Has anyone ever asked you how we win the world for Christ? How do we convince others that there is nothing in this world that compares to living for Christ? The way we win the world is to die to self. Christ modeled this throughout his ministry.

As referenced in the last chapter, in Philippians 2, Paul gives us a picture of Jesus as one who has died to himself, by describing Jesus in this way: "...who, though he was in the form of God, did not count equality with God a thing to be grasped, but emptied himself, by taking the form of a servant, being born in the likeness of men. And being found in human form, he humbled himself by becoming obedient to the point of death, even death on a cross" (Philippians 2:6-8). This is the perfect example of dying to self.

Jesus is God—the Creator and Sustainer of the universe. But He let go of all of His own nature and rights as the King of Kings, and He came to earth as a human. Most importantly, he was not even a noble or important human but was a villager, a carpenter—an average, everyday human without wealth or stature. And if this weren't enough, He allowed Himself to be killed in an unjust, horrible manner befitting a criminal. He died, but His physical death was just the final step of an Earthly life filled with choice after choice to die to Himself by releasing all of His rights. Every single thing He did was to glorify His Father, never to elevate Himself. This is the example He set for us.

The greatest need for us as Christ-following men is to rid ourselves of our carnality, our worldliness. The solution is not to have men move *toward* the cross but to get them *on* the cross! That is, we must embrace dying to self and being alive in Christ. The uncrucified life has no productive power. If he fails to associate with the Lord Jesus in His death, the believer must concede to defeat and admit that he is barren, sterile, and unfruitful. We become powerless when we allow different gods to occupy our time.

How do we become more Christlike? Starting from the premise that our primary area of influence in life is our family, what does this mean for us? It means we must die to ourselves when loving our families. Being the leaders of our families does not mean being the rulers of our wives and children. Remember the words in the passage we just read from Philippians 2:7: "…but emptied himself, by taking the form of a servant." We are to be servants to our wives and children.

What do you think you deserve as the husband and father in your home? Do you deserve to be served after a long day of work? As Scripture guides us, this is not the case. Instead, come home with an attitude of wanting to serve your family. Do you deserve to have your wife clean the house and cook dinner because you are earning the money? As Scripture guides us, this is not the case. Instead, come home and make dinner for her. Do you deserve to have your children listen to you talk about your day? As Scripture guides us, this is not the case. Instead, ask them about theirs. Do you deserve to unwind in front of the television? As Scripture guides us, this is not the case. Instead, engage your family in a discussion about God's Word. Dying to self is not easy, but it is the example our Lord gave us and it is far more rewarding than any other approach.

Just like the Kingdom of God, the vision of Malachi Dads advances through the humble, daily "deaths" of men who die quietly for their children and wives because of their faith in Christ. There is no fanfare. There are no parades. Many of them are nameless—just like you, just like me. This is not about power or prestige. It is about being humble men of faith who pass our love of God to our families. We put them first in all things.

Where do we start?

Pray.

When people are dead in their sins, only God can turn their hearts from stone to living flesh. So we must come to Him first. As fathers we must come before the living God and earnestly beseech Him for His grace, mercy, and favor to be upon us and our families. We cry out for His mercy in our lives and in the lives of our family members.

As fathers we must pray constantly for the spiritual growth of each of our family members. Only through God's regenerating power of His Holy Spirit can they begin to know God and respond to Him. On behalf of your family, pray earnestly, deeply, and regularly for God to move in their lives.

Be in His Word.

If we are going to be the men of God that we are called to be, we cannot depend on Sunday preaching to grow our faith. We need to study God's Word on our own. We need to use whatever methods we can to help us to understand, know, and love His Word. We have so many resources at our fingertips; there is no excuse to not study the Bible.

Unfortunately, as a body of believers we seem to be biblically illiterate, but it should be quite the opposite! Our children should come to Sunday School equipped and prepared because of our teaching and training at home. They should already know a great deal. Even if they are very young, tell your children Bible stories. As they grow, read the Bible with and to them. Help them to memorize Scripture with you. We need to put God's Word in our hearts, and we must help our children to do the same.

Seek His face.

1 Chronicles 16:11 says, "Seek the LORD and His strength; seek His presence continually." In His strength, we can become the spiritual leaders that He created us to be. But we must be disciplined to do so. What we need as fathers is to continually cry out to our God to change us and to mold us. 2 Chronicles 7:14 is a familiar verse: "If my people who are called by my name humble themselves,

and pray and seek my face and turn from their wicked ways, then I will hear from heaven and will forgive their sin and heal their land."

What are we being called to do? To believe what the Bible says. To believe it so much that we obey it and live for Him. To humble ourselves. To pray. To seek His face. To turn from our ways. Then, and only then, He will hear, forgive, and heal—our land, our souls, and our families.

Put Christ first. Put your family second. Put others third. And go forth in the power of His love.

Our culture will beckon to you and tell you that dying to self is silly. It will tell you that you must have time for yourself. But that's not Scripture's calling for us.

Yes, you might get tired. You might burn out from time to time. But we need to remember great men of the faith. We admire the apostle Paul and men like Jonathan Edwards, A.W. Tozer, and C.H. Spurgeon. But we are often hesitant to pay the price they paid—the price by being men who walked alone, who lived with God, and who loved His Word. They were men, though not perfect, who sought to die to self.

Christ enabled them to pick up their cross and follow Him. Dying to self looks different for all of us because we all have different life situations, but the overarching goal is the same—we make it our aim to glorify God by doing His will in everything.

R.C. Sproul Jr., from *Dying Daily*

As I type this, my dear wife and mother to our eight children is battling leukemia. This is, in fact, her third battle with the scourge of cancer in the past seven years. Joyfully, once again, it seems the enemy is in retreat and we are in the closing months of the war. While my wife is fighting death, however, I have found myself not just frightened but bewildered. What is it that I am supposed to do?

The logistics are hard enough—how to get her to her appointments, make supper, shuttle the kids to practices, and also fulfill my own calling in the Kingdom. But compared to ministering to my family, the logistics are easy. The far greater challenge has been discovering how to comfort my bride in her pain and fear and comforting my children in their fear and confusion. And, of course, dealing with my own emotional turmoil.

Having been touched by the Malachi Dads program and having seen godly men in profoundly difficult circumstances seeking to minister to their own children, I remember my calling. This circumstance is not so unusual. God's Word does not give answers to husbands with healthy wives but leave men like me in the dark. The commands of Christ, which are in turn the law of perfect liberty, are as much mine as they ever were. If my wife is fighting death, what am I supposed to do? I am supposed to die. I am supposed to die to self, to sacrifice all the little things that mean far too much to me. I am supposed to stop worrying about myself, to let the dead bury the dead.

We all have small things in our lives. They begin only as little treats we give ourselves, little blessings that we look forward to as the day rolls on. It may be a quick side trip for an ice cream sundae. It may be watching your favorite sports team play. It may even be reading a chapter or two of that detective novel just before bed. These are, or can be, good things. Little pleasures come to us from our big God, because He loves us. Whether you eat ice cream or root for the Pittsburgh Steelers, you can do all things as unto the Lord.

The trouble comes when we treat these gifts as our due, when we come to think we deserve them. We begin to crave them and so resent when our wives, children, or various circumstances get in the way of these delights. Suddenly we feel cheated, not just by the events in our lives, but by the One who ordains those events. We think there is something wrong with the universe, that it is broken. And in our prayers we begin to complain to The Management.

Dead men, however, have no complaints. They have no expectations. Dead men never grumble that they are not getting their due. Do you remember when you died? When you came face to face with your sins, when you were overwhelmed with your guilt, when you clung to the cross of Christ, when you were brought into union with Him? At that moment you were crucified with Him. You embraced death, thus entered into life by saying to our Lord, "Whatever you have for me, I will accept. I will go where you send me. I will obey what you command. All that I have, and all that I am are yours." Do you remember that day?

That was the day you volunteered for the job of loving, comforting, and encouraging a sick wife. That was the day you signed up to pour your time and energy into the children He put in your care. That was day you laid ice cream and football games and detective novels at the foot of the cross, right beside the foolish notion that even a slice of your time was your own.

And this, this is the day when you find out that as sweet as ice cream is, it will never be as sweet as kissing your wife's bald head. This is the day you find out that tossing a football in the backyard with your boys will always beat watching the Steelers win the Super Bowl. This is the day when the mystery story is solved, when you find out who dunnit; it was Jesus that killed you so that He might make you alive.

I'm still learning to die. I practice every day. One day I'll get it right, and He will be there to congratulate me, to greet me.

CONCLUSION

Live It Out

Most men, even Christian men, are relationally passive in their homes. They leave the spiritual training of their children to the church or Christian programs. They may not think of it at all! Many men work long hours, rationalizing it by saying that they are showing their love by providing for their families. But if you are an absent or passive father, or even if you are present and active but not relating to your family in God's love, you are not providing what your family needs most.

You now have a vision of what it is to be a Malachi Dad. You have seen what God has done through normal, ordinary fathers who became Malachi Dads.

What will you do with this?

If God has used this book to help you look at yourself in the mirror, don't do what James warns against in James 1:23-24: "For if anyone is a hearer of the word and not a doer, he is like a man who looks intently at his natural face in a mirror. For he looks at himself and goes away and at once forgets what he was like." Do more than just look at yourself—take action!

Our families need us. Your family needs you. They need you to build a strong, vibrant legacy in Christ Jesus. They need you to own your God-given role and responsibilities as leader of the home. They need for you to live a transformed life in Christ—an authentic, deep faith that dominates your life. They need you to realize your poverty before God and seek the Lord's salvation and sanctification by the power of the Gospel in your heart and life. They need you to die to yourself daily.

The answer is not a list of how-tos or a great program. The answer is Christ exalted in you, and passing that down to your children. It is obedience to God's ordained structure of authority—the structure that makes you not "king of the home" but "servant of the home."

A servant is humble. We must be humble. A good servant looks for ways to serve others. We must serve like that. By putting Christ first and seeking His face, we will live in His strength, not ours, and this will bring humility and servant-hood to our homes through us.

Just as Christ weaved bright colors into the tapestry of my life, pray for Him to do the same in your life and the life of your family. But we must do more than just pray. That tapestry is made up by a series of decisions – ones that weave dark colors of darkness and despair, or bright colors of life and legacy. God provides the guidance; you make the moves.

Whom will you honor?

Questions for Reflection and Discussion

Introduction

What do you think about the idea of tapestry?

What are some of the colors that have been woven into your life thus far?

What role can you play in changing the colors from darkness to light?

Chapter 1

What legacy have you received thus far?

How do you want to be remembered after you're gone?

What are you doing to try to intentionally build that legacy?

Chapter 2

Have you embraced your personal responsibility as the spiritual leader of your family?

What does this practically look like for you?

What do you need to do to increase your focus on living up to your responsibility?

Chapter 3

How focused on God is your life?

What do your wife, children, and others see in your life?

What actions do you need to make to change what others see coming from your life?

Chapter 4

Have you recognized the depth of your sin?

Have you turned from your sin and entrusted your life to Christ?

What action steps do you need to make on a regular basis to live in light of your poverty before God?

Chapter 5

Have you trusted Christ for your salvation?

Does your life with Christ reflect an ongoing relationship or one focused only on avoiding hell?

How has this chapter confirmed or challenged your understanding of the Gospel?

Chapter 6

How are you dying to self on a daily basis?

How can others continue to help or challenge you to live in this selfless way?

How is your life of prayer? Of being in God's Word? Of seeking His face?

Conclusion

How have you been encouraged or challenged as a result of this book and the stories in it?

What personal action steps do you need to take to live life more as a Malachi Dad?

Who do you need to start selflessly investing your time in to help change a generation and build a legacy of faith in Christ?

A Malachi Dad is a man who loves God and glorifies Him by building a legacy of faith in Christ within his family first, then challenging other men to do the same in theirs.

A Malachi Dad is a man who embraces his God-given roles and responsibilities as the spiritual leader of his family.

A Malachi Dad is a man who embraces the power of a transformed life in Christ for his family to see and emulate.

A Malachi Dad is a man who knows how poor and dependent he is before God.

A Malachi Dad is a man who lives by the Gospel, being aware daily of his need for salvation and sanctification.

A Malachi Dad is a man who dies to self, daily.